MAKING
MONEY
WORK

The Teens' Guide to Saving, Investing, and Building Wealth

by KARA McGUIRE

COMPASS POINT BOOKS
a capstone imprint

Compass Point Books are published by Capstone,
1710 Roe Crest Drive, North Mankato, Minnesota 56003
www.capstonepub.com

Editorial Credits
Angie Kaelberer and Catherine Neitge, editors; Ted Williams, designer;
Eric Gohl, media researcher; Laura Manthe, production specialist

Image Credits
Corbis: K.J. Historical, 57; Courtesy of Therese R. Nicklas: 23; Flickr:
Joseph, 29; Shutterstock: Andresr, 34, 59, Ariwasabi, 24, Artisticco, 14–15,
brinkstock, 33, Georgios Kollidas, 28, Golden Pixels LLC, 53, hfng, cover,
Horiyan, 17 (top), Iaroslav Neliubov, 9, iris 42, 36, Luis Viegas, 17 (bottom),
lukeruk, 19, Mackey Creations, 13, Michal Durinik, 44, mj007, 1, Mmaxer,
39, mypokcik, 46–47, photastic, 20–21, Renewer, 54, Robyn Mackenzie, 30,
sheelamohanachandran2010, 41, Steve Cukrov, 42–43, Stuart Jenner, 4–5,
Syda Productions, 7, szefei, 51, ventdusud, 26–27, Vladru, 10–11, zentilia,
17 (middle)

Design Elements: Shutterstock

Library of Congress Cataloging-in-Publication Data
McGuire, Kara.
  Making money work : the teens' guide to saving, investing, and building
wealth / by Kara McGuire.
     pages cm.—(Compass point books. Financial literacy)
  Includes bibliographical references and index.
  ISBN 978-0-7565-4922-0 (library binding)
  ISBN 978-0-7565-4931-2 (paperback)
  ISBN 978-0-7565-4939-8 (eBook PDF)
  1. Finance, Personal—Juvenile literature. 2. Investments—Juvenile literature.
  3. Teenagers—Finance, Personal—Juvenile literature. I. Title.
  HG179.M38325 2015
  332.60835—dc23   2014003740

Printed in Canada.
032014   008086FRF14

MAKE IT A HABIT

From the time we're old enough to understand that money buys toys, movies, and the latest must-have pair of jeans, we are ready to shop. There are so many desirable things to have. When we walk by stores, check out online photos of what our friends bought at the mall, or see a celebrity carrying a certain smartphone or wearing designer sunglasses, our brains shout, "I want, I want, I want!"

It would be so easy to spend all of our money on new things and good times. One of the most important things to learn as you get older, gain responsibilities, and have access to more money is the importance of saving. There are many places, ways, and reasons to save. It can be overwhelming, but don't worry. This book will help you understand the basics of accumulating cash. And the sooner you make saving a habit, the richer you'll be.

CHAPTER ONE

SAVVY
SAVING

Pay yourself first. Maybe you've heard this simple phrase before. But what does it mean? When you get your paycheck, before you cover your cell phone bill or make plans to go out with friends, set aside some money in savings. That's what it means.

Paying yourself first is a way to put your financial security before your wants. Try to keep the cost of your needs low enough that you can pay yourself first, cover your expenses, and still have fun.

But there's more to saving than just deciding to put money away. You must decide where to save, what you are saving for, and when you will need to access the money.

WHY SAVE?

Let's face it. Saving probably is not the first thing you'd like to do with your money, but it's necessary. We save money to afford purchases we plan to make. Some of those purchases will be for things we want and some for things we need. But we also save money to plan for the unexpected.

When you save money, you give up the opportunity to do something else with it, such as spend it or give it away. This is known as opportunity cost.

Because saving isn't the most fun thing in the world, many of us need to come up with ways to persuade us to save. For some, the security of having money "just in case" is incentive enough. For others, it's the challenge of meeting a goal. Then there are those who are driven to save because they like to see their fortune grow or not have to ask their parents for money to buy a new phone. As in most financial decisions, people have very different ideas about how to manage their savings. They come up with reasons and amounts to save based on their wants and needs.

Putting your goals in order

If only there was unlimited money, like a pot of gold at the end of the rainbow. But since there isn't, you need to decide what to save for and how much you can afford to set aside for that goal. Chances are you have more than one savings goal. You might want to save for a new video game, a spring break trip, car insurance, and college tuition. And while you might not be thrilled with the idea, it's wise to start saving for retirement now.

How do you figure out how to save for everything? First you determine how much money you have to save after paying for today's needs and wants. Then it's a matter of dividing up the money that's left. Financial experts suggest trying to save at least 10 percent of your income for retirement. Some say you need to save 20 percent to be safe. If that's too much, start small. Even $20 a month will add up over time.

9

WHERE TO SAVE?

Banks accept deposits of money from customers. They also lend money to customers. Banks are for-profit institutions and charge interest to people taking out loans. They also may pay interest to people depositing money, depending on what type of account they have. Interest is your payment for allowing the bank to lend your money to other customers.

The interest is calculated as a percentage based on how much money you've deposited.

General savings accounts are designed to save for all sorts of reasons. Other accounts are designed to save for particular goals, such as college and retirement. These specialized accounts tend to have tax benefits. But they also tend to have restrictions on how you can use them, so you need to be sure before you open one that you won't need the money for something else.

Savings account: A savings account is versatile, easy to access, and designed to save money for any purpose. But because the interest rate earned is low, it's best for emergency savings and short-term savings goals.

IRA: IRA stands for individual retirement account. It has tax advantages that lower your tax bill today. It can be used in some circumstances for a home down payment or college tuition, but it's mainly considered a retirement account.

401(k), 403(b), 457 plans: Various workplace retirement plans are set up for you by your employer. You designate a percentage of your paycheck to go into that account. Some employers will contribute a matching amount to the account, usually up to a certain percentage.

529 plans: Savers use 529 plans to save for college. They must be used for college expenses.

ROTH IRA: A Roth IRA is funded with money left after you pay taxes. It can only be funded with money you earn from working. It's designed to lower your tax bill in the future. This fund is much more versatile than the IRA, because you can withdraw the money you contribute to the fund for any purpose at any time. This makes it good for saving for retirement, college, or a house. And if you don't tap it for other purposes, you will have money for retirement. It's like the little black dress of savings.

Brokerage accounts: Brokerage accounts let you invest in any number of things—from individual stocks to mutual funds. These accounts can be used for any purpose.

Emergency savings: Rainy day fund. Cash cushion. These are terms used to describe money you save just in case something unexpected or unfortunate happens. An emergency savings account should be opened at a bank or credit union and should not be used as fun money, even if you're tempted.

What are some examples of acceptable expenses for this type of account? Paying for an unexpectedly high heating bill in your first apartment. Replacing a lost textbook. Repairing a bike tire. But while it's OK to use this type of account to fix items you own, repairs aren't exactly emergencies. You should anticipate and budget for the cost of repairs and routine maintenance of bikes, appliances, cars, and homes. So how much emergency savings should you have? If you're just getting started, pick an achievable goal—$1,000, $500, or even $50—and an amount to save from each paycheck or allowance. It's OK to start small.

WHEN TO SAVE

Some places to save are better than others, depending on when you'll need the money. This is called your time horizon. Before picking your account, you must ask yourself whether you need your money very soon (in the next year), in the short term (less than three years), medium term (three to five years), or long term (five or more years). This will help you decide whether to save in a bank account or to take on more risk by investing your money in stocks.

short term

medium term

long term

Bet you didn't think physics had any application to saving, did you? But the law of inertia—that objects at rest tend to stay at rest and objects in motion tend to stay in motion—can be the difference between retiring one day and working until you drop. Inertia is derived from the Latin word *iners*, which means idle or lazy. What behavioral economists have found is that inertia can be a positive force in savings, but only if you can manage to get started.

Let's say you just landed your first job. Your employer will ask you where you want to deposit your paycheck. It's typical to divide your paycheck into more than one account, such as a checking account and a savings account. You could decide to have 10 percent of your salary automatically deposited into a savings account each month. Or you could decide to put money in a savings account on your own if you have money left over after paying expenses. Which choice increases your odds of successfully saving? You guessed it—the first choice. By setting up your paycheck so you automatically save each payday, you are using inertia to your benefit. If you say you'll take care of it later, you may never get around to setting up that savings account.

It can be challenging, but it's important to get into the habit of saving. The earlier you do, the better. As you get older, you'll likely encounter unexpected expenses, and you will need a cash cushion to ensure a soft landing.

Your grandparents probably tell stories about how items cost a lot less when they were young, such as candy bars that sold for a nickel. You'd have a hard time finding a candy bar for that price today. Prices for goods and services increase over time. That's called inflation, and it can take a big bite out of your long-term savings. What cost $100 in 1993 costs about $162 today. A $100 bill in 1913 has the same buying power as $2,359 today. With luck, your salary will increase to keep up with inflation, but this isn't always the case. Inflation is just one reason why it's necessary to save.

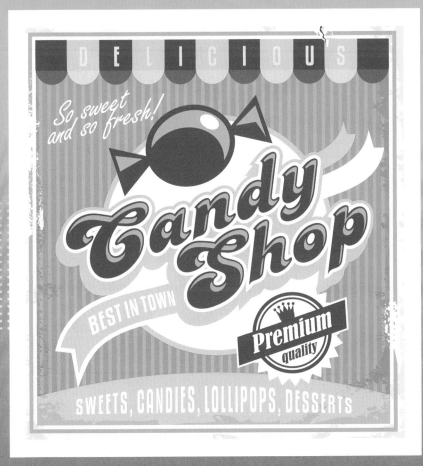

SAVINGS IN DISGUISE

You can positively punch up your bottom line in more ways than just sticking money in the bank. For example, when you pay off debt, you are essentially saving money. If you pay off a loan that charges 5 percent interest, you've just saved yourself the 5 percent you would have had to pay in the future on that loan.

Another way to save money is by spending less. Instead of buying an item the moment you see it, research prices and look for coupons. The less you pay, the more money you've saved. Finally, there's the choice to not buy something in the first place. Many wants fade if you decide to sit on a purchase for a while.

PATIENCE + PERSEVERANCE = FULL POCKETBOOK!

That is financial planner Therese R. Nicklas' equation for financial success.

What does this mean? Nicklas says in order to succeed at achieving financial goals, you need two key ingredients—patience and perseverance. "Patience means before making a purchase, give yourself the 24-hour test. Wait 24 hours before buying something. If the craving passes, you really didn't need the item. Persevere and keep your eye on the prize!"

Break your goal down to manageable pieces, says Nicklas, a Boston-area certified financial planner. She gives this example: Say you have a goal of joining your high school class on a European trip. The cost is $1,800. It is September 1, and you just learned of this opportunity. The trip will take place in April, and you need to have your final payment in by March 31. EVERYONE is going.

You approach your parents with your best sales pitch, and they say flat out, "No, we can't afford it. College is right around the corner!" So what do you do? Give up, keep begging, hoping to wear them down, or figure out how to raise the money yourself? Let's hope you choose the latter, and here is what you will need to do. It is as easy as 1, 2, 3!

Our imaginary high school student can follow Nicklas' three-part plan to raise money for the trip.

1. Create a timeline. You have seven months to raise $1,800, which equals about $257 per month. Looking at it another way, you have 30 weeks to raise $1,800, which equals $60 per week.

In order to net $60 per week, you would need to work approximately 10 hours a week and earn approximately $8 per hour. (Don't forget tax withholding.) If you have other expenses besides your trip, you will need to earn more to cover them.

2. Get a job and create a savings plan. A

part-time job after school and on weekends should cover your needs. What special skills do you have that could earn you money? Love kids? How about babysitting? Lawn mowing, computer repair (or computer lessons), tutoring? A job in retail? Put on your thinking cap and let your imagination soar!

You know you need to save a minimum of $60 per week to achieve your goal. Set up a separate bank account for the trip. Either set up an automatic deposit to this account, or discipline yourself to go to the bank each week and make your deposit.

Your patience and perseverance will pay off! In no time you will see your bank account grow. Before you know it, you will be enjoying your European trip with the satisfaction that you did it yourself!

3. Create a lifestyle plan. Now that you achieved

this milestone, keep going. Don't stop!

Continue to save for other future goals, such as buying a car or contributing to your college education. Having a separate bank account for special goals makes it easier to discipline yourself to succeed.

You just taught yourself two valuable skills—paying yourself first, and living within your means. Congratulations! You are on your way to enjoying a lifestyle of financial freedom!

HOW I SAVED FOR
A TRIP TO EUROPE

Josie Smith, a 13-year-old from suburban St. Paul, Minnesota, explains how she saved for a trip:

"This summer I went to the Czech Republic, Hungary, and Transylvania. I went with my church to our sister church. The trip cost about $3,450.

"I knew that I would have to pay for some of the trip and that my parents would pay for a lot of it and my grandparents would help. My parents paid for the plane tickets and for some money for a hotel for a few nights. I paid $800 ($600 for the rest of

the trip, plus the spending money, which was $200.) My grandparents gave me $200 specifically for my train ticket from Prague to Budapest. I also got a $1,000 scholarship from my church.

"To earn money I babysat at church and for other kids and saved my birthday money. I also have been cat-sitting since second grade. I'm a saver, so I already had a lot of money in my bank account—about $300—and saving is just a natural thing that I do. My top piece of advice for tweens and teens trying to save for something big is don't go to the mall that often, or places where you can be easily tempted to buy something.

"Also think 'Do I really need this; will I use it?' and if you won't, then don't buy it."

"A penny saved is a penny earned."

"For age and want, save while you may, no morning sun lasts a whole day."

"A small leak will sink a great ship."

Benjamin Franklin is best known as one of America's Founding Fathers, signer of the Declaration of Independence, publisher of *Poor Richard's Almanac*, and inventor of bifocals. But did you know he could be considered America's first financial guru?

As a newspaperman and printer, Franklin shared many common-sense words of wisdom about saving, earning, and spending money. Many of the sayings are laid out in his 1758 essay *The Way to Wealth*. Do his quotes sound familiar?

The abandoned Wyndcliffe mansion on the Hudson River may have inspired the saying "Keeping up with the Joneses." Built in 1853, its first owner was Elizabeth Schermerhorn Jones.

KEEPING UP WITH THE JONESES

When people say they are "keeping up with the Joneses," they are comparing their lifestyle and possessions to those of their neighbors. Some say the idea of the Joneses came from a comic strip of the same name published in the early 1900s. Others say the phrase may have come from a wealthy New York family of that name in the mid-1800s.

Either way, trying to keep up with the stuff and spending habits of your friends and neighbors can get you into a lot of financial trouble. Besides, there's no way of knowing if your classmates or neighbors bought a new car outright or with a high-interest loan they can barely afford.

PEER PRESSURE AND SAVING

We've all experienced peer pressure at some point in our lives. Usually it's a negative influence, but peer pressure can be put to good use if you and your friends are supporting one another's financial goals. For example, the app PiggyMojo pairs you with a friend to help you spend less on small things that don't seem like a big deal but can add up to big money over time. If you buy a $4 smoothie five days a week, that amounts to roughly $1,000 a year.

Here's how PiggyMojo works: After signing up for a free account, pick a goal, such as buying fewer smoothies. Pick a friend who will support your new goal. Every time you avoid temptation and choose not to buy a smoothie, text PiggyMojo the cost and name of what you didn't buy. PiggyMojo texts your partner and tracks your savings. You can then transfer that money into your savings account and watch it grow over time.

CHAPTER TWO

TAKING IT
TO THE BANK

A piggy bank is a fine place to start saving. But at some point your savings will outgrow a ceramic pig. Instead of getting an even bigger piggy bank, most people trade up to the real thing—a bank.

Putting your money in the bank is safer than keeping it at home. It's also harder to spend your money if it's not right within reach. Banks also give you lots of choices for how to save and access your money.

Your parents may have opened a savings account for you when you were young and deposited gift money into that account. The account was probably at their bank, because having your account there was convenient for them.

CHOOSING A BANK

When you're ready to start managing your own money, think about what's important to you in a financial institution. All banks have FDIC insurance, which means that up to $250,000 of your deposits are guaranteed, even in the rare event that the bank would fail. All banks provide checks, access to ATMs, and debit cards. Nearly all banks have online tools to help you keep track of your money and where it goes.

The options of checking your account balance with a text message and using an app to deposit birthday checks with your smartphone may make a bank located near you seem less important.

While some people like to have a bank location, called a branch, near their home, workplace, or school, fewer people visit bank branches today than in the past. If you like to handle your banking online or by smartphone, a nearby location may be less important than a bank with the latest online and mobile banking tools.

Some banks offer new customers incentives for opening an account and keeping it open for a certain period of time. Banks used to give items such as toasters as account-opening gifts. Today the gifts are more likely to be cash or gift cards. If you're having a tough time deciding between financial institutions, consider one that gives you a bonus for opening the account. Some banks will give you $100 for opening a new account and depositing money. That will give you a head start toward your savings goals.

CREDIT UNIONS

Opening an account at a bank isn't your only option. Like a bank, a credit union keeps your money safe, provides access to your money when needed, and offers loans. But credit unions are not-for-profit, and the users of a credit union are its members who typically have a vote in some credit union decisions.

Credit unions tend to be smaller, locally run, and may limit who becomes a member. For example, you might have to live in a particular community or work at a certain company. Whether you pick a bank or a credit union is up to you. Either way, your money will be safe.

THE MAGIC OF COMPOUND INTEREST

Various types of interest calculations determine how much money you will earn on the money in your account. The most basic calculation is simple interest, which is calculated only on the money you initially deposited in the account.

To earn more on your money, open an account that pays interest using compound interest. With compound interest, you earn interest on the cash in your account and on any interest you've previously earned. The more often your bank calculates your compound interest, the faster your money will multiply. An account compounding interest four times a year is better than an account that compounds once each year.

For doing nothing but keeping your money in the bank, you earn money. Without lifting a finger. And every time you are paid interest, the amount of interest paid gets bigger. This is why it's so important to start saving for retirement as soon as you can. Your money will start small but grow sizably over time.

Compound interest plays a big role in being able to retire. Your money has more chances to compound if you start saving for retirement decades before you plan to stop working. It may seem crazy to put money away for retirement when you're still saving for your first car or paying for college. But you'd be crazy *not* to do it.

The tale of
TWO SAVERS

Tammy and Jerry are friends who are 65 years old and share a birthday. When Tammy was 25, she started an IRA and saved $100 a month for 40 years. The IRA produced average returns of 7 percent per year.

Jerry waited until he was 45 years old and doubled the contributions, putting aside $200 per month for 20 years. Both friends stopped saving on their 65th birthdays. Without calculating interest, the two friends saved an identical amount: $48,000. But when factoring in compound interest, who comes out ahead?

Tammy does. By a lot. Just by starting 20 years earlier and letting compound interest work its magic over a longer time period, Tammy ends up with $258,020. Jerry has just a little more than $103,000. The lesson: starting early with any dollar amount is smarter than waiting until you have enough money to save a larger amount.

CHAPTER THREE

INVESTING
BASICS

Investing can be a daunting topic for beginners, but it's really quite simple. The basic concept of investing is taking the money you have now and making it grow.

You can start with as little as $20 and can invest for many reasons—for the challenge, for the sense of owning something, or for the more practical purpose of making sure you have enough money in the future.

Generally, investments will earn you more than money sitting in a savings account will. Investments are also designed for a time horizon that lasts years, not months. Some investments are riskier than others. Some investments are liquid, meaning it's easy to get your money out of the investment relatively quickly. Others are illiquid, meaning your money will be tough to access.

The return on an investment—what you get for investing the time or money in the first place—is not always measured in an exact dollar amount. For example, your education is an investment. Research shows that a four-year college degree is worth an average of more than $1 million in earning potential.

TYPES OF INVESTMENTS

STOCKS

Stocks allow people to buy small pieces, called shares, of a company. Companies sell stock to raise money for various purposes. The shares are bought and sold on a marketplace called an exchange. Most of the buying and selling a century ago took place on the stock market floor, but today most transactions occur electronically.

The value of stock shares can go up and down. It's possible to lose all of your money invested in a stock. But on average the stock market has increased in value.

When you own stock in a company, you are called a shareholder. You have a vested interest in how well the company does. When a company does well, its stock tends to go up, which means your shares are worth more if you were to sell them that day. If a company doesn't perform as well as expected, the value of the shares can go down, and your investment would be worth less. Since money invested in the stock market should have a longer time horizon, you should not worry if the market fluctuates. It only matters how much the stock is worth on the day you plan to sell it.

BONDS

A bond is essentially an IOU given to you by the company that sells the bond. When you buy a bond, the company agrees to pay back the money you loaned plus interest on a certain date in the future. Some bonds are riskier than others and depend on the overall health of a company's finances. Bonds are considered safer than stocks, but it is possible to lose money on bonds.

MUTUAL FUNDS

A mutual fund is a collection of various types of investments. Think of it as a grocery bag that holds each of your financial food groups—a mix of stocks, bonds, and cash. Professional investors manage some mutual funds, charging fees to choose what goes in the grocery bag. They hope to fill it with investments that will grow the most over time. Other mutual funds track an index of stocks or bonds, buying a little bit of all the stocks or bonds on the index. Because these mutual funds, called index funds, don't have professionals picking the stocks or bonds to buy, index funds have lower fees.

SAVINGS BONDS

Chances are you've received a savings bond as a gift at some point in your life. The U.S. government sells the bonds to raise money. Savings bonds carry little risk, but their interest rate tends to be low.

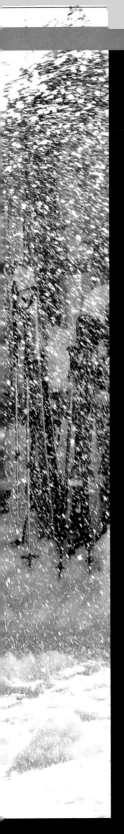

PROPERTY

Investing opportunities exist outside of financial accounts. It isn't necessary to have millions of dollars in order to invest in a company or product. You could buy property. There are other types of property to buy besides a home or piece of land. You could invest in a snowblower and start a business clearing snow or renting the machine to neighbors. Or you can invest in a friend's business, trading money for a piece of the profits or some other benefit.

INVESTING IN OTHERS

Crowdfunding is a way for people to invest small sums in interesting projects and businesses. Websites such as Kickstarter.com allow people to contribute money to start-up projects such as making a film, starting a fashion company, or inventing a new app. Investors usually receive a gift of appreciation in return, which varies depending on the amount of the investment.

DIVERSIFICATION

Don't put all your eggs in one basket! That old saying is a favorite to dust off when talking about investing. It means that you should not put all of your money in a single investment. Doing so is risky because if something happens to that investment, you could lose everything.

For example, you might really love hamburgers from a certain restaurant chain and decide to become part owner of that company by purchasing shares of its stock. But you wouldn't want to spend every penny you have on stock in this company. People may decide the burgers are unhealthy or don't taste good. Or the price of beef could skyrocket. That would hurt the restaurant and cause its stock price, and your investment, to decline in value.

The concept of putting your money in multiple types of investments is called diversification. To stick with the egg metaphor, diversification prevents all of your eggs from breaking if you stumble or the bottom falls out of a basket. With eggs spread out in several types of baskets, you take less risk and increase the chance that your money will be there for you, no matter what happens.

RISKY BUSINESS

Investments have various degrees of risk. Stock in a new company that is based overseas is riskier than money saved in a savings account at a bank. Taking greater risks can yield greater returns. But the losses can be greater as well.

Risk is not always about losing money. There is also the risk that money will grow too slowly to keep up with inflation or to reach your goals within your desired time frame.

We're used to a certain amount of risk in day-to-day life. How well each of us deals with risk depends on many factors. It's smart before deciding how to invest your money to figure out what's called your risk tolerance. There are many risk tolerance questionnaires you can try out online. One such quiz, developed by two university personal finance professors, asks such questions as:

You are on a TV game show and can choose one of the following. Which would you take?

$1,000 in cash
A 50% chance at winning $5,000
A 25% chance at winning $10,000
A 5% chance at winning $100,000

Suppose a relative left you an inheritance of $100,000, stipulating in the will that you invest ALL the money in ONE of the following choices. Which one would you select?

A savings account or money market mutual fund
A mutual fund that owns stocks and bonds
A portfolio of 15 common stocks
Commodities like gold, silver, and oil

Quiz source: http://njaes.rutgers.edu/money/riskquiz/

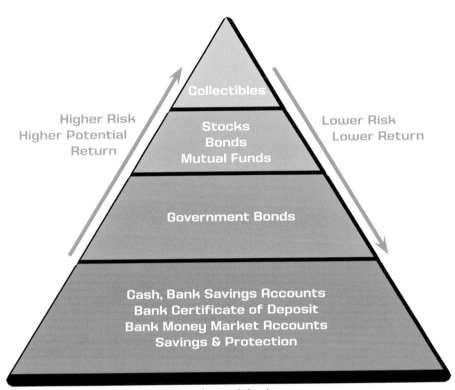

Higher Risk
Higher Potential
Return

Lower Risk
Lower Return

Collectibles

Stocks
Bonds
Mutual Funds

Government Bonds

Cash, Bank Savings Accounts
Bank Certificate of Deposit
Bank Money Market Accounts
Savings & Protection

Source: http://themint.org/kids/risk-and-rewards.html

REDUCE RISK

Investors can use diversification to reduce risk by varying the types of investments, such as stocks, bonds, cash, and property. When you'll need to access your money is also important so you won't need to take it out all at once.

It's hard to figure out what funds to set aside for the future without mapping what the future might bring. Like a road trip, you don't know exactly what you'll encounter along the way. There could be an accident, unexpected costs from a car breakdown, or the cost of a coffee needed for a jolt of energy. But part of planning is making educated guesses about what your life will look like and what financial needs you can estimate.

You'll need to figure out the right balance between saving, investing, spending, and donating. Finding this balance depends on your values, expenses, and goals.

Most experts suggest that if you have a retirement plan at your workplace, take advantage of it. Ideally, you'd be able to save 10 to 15 percent of your income. But if that's too much, at least save enough so that you qualify for any matching money your employer gives you. Typically, that's around 3 percent of your wages. Also save a small amount in an emergency savings fund. Experts suggest three to six months worth of bare-bones living expenses—think ramen noodles, not fancy restaurant meals. Or set a dollar-based goal, such as $10 per paycheck until you get to $100. Finally, think about opening a Roth IRA account, which is a great place to save for retirement because your money grows tax-free for life.

Both workplace retirement accounts and Roth IRAs give you incentives to save. If your employer contributes money to your workplace 401(k) plan provided you save a certain amount, that is an incentive.

The tax benefits of choosing to save in a workplace retirement plan, a Roth IRA account, or in a 529 plan for college are incentives because the less money you owe the Internal Revenue Service, the more you get to keep. And it's important both at the individual level and for society as a whole to have people who are financially secure and prepared for whatever comes their way.

WHAT TO DO?

If you have a chunk of money, should you invest it all at once or over time? Depends. The argument for investing all at once is that the total amount of your money is fully invested for a longer period of time. The argument for investing a little bit at regular intervals is that you will invest at different price points. Because markets and investment prices fluctuate, if you purchase a bit at a time, it will balance out the points when you pay more or less for a share. That is sometimes referred to as buying high or low. This idea of investing a little at a time is called dollar-cost averaging. It is the common method for investing in workplace retirement plans.

GETTING ADVICE

Is your head spinning yet? Investing overwhelms many adults, so don't worry if it takes time to make sense of it all. Some people use a financial adviser to help them make financial decisions. Advisers go by various names—financial adviser, financial planner, broker, or wealth manager. Depending on their training and licensing, they may have special titles such as certified financial planner (CFP) or chartered life underwriter (CLU).

Financial advisers make investments and give financial advice, but they don't work for free. Some advisers earn a fee based on how much money they invest. Others earn commission based on the types of products they sell. You need to understand the fees you are charged for advice, because fees can take a big bite out of your return.

People don't typically start working with a financial adviser until their financial lives become more complicated, and they have more money to invest. Many adults choose to manage their own financial affairs throughout life. It's common for teens to turn to people they know, such as their parents or guardians, for help with money matters. Websites and books can also help. But you need to understand the investments you are buying, even if you have someone knowledgeable to help you. Smart people have lost life savings to smooth-talking salespeople who have promised too-good-to-be-true returns from investments.

Super-sized Stocks

If you invested some of your money in companies instead of spending it on the goods they make, you could make big bucks.

Share price in May 1999	Share price in May 2014
McDonalds $27.61	$100.96
Apple $10.59	$594.41
Disney $23.87	$79.56
Nike $13.09	$72.92

MANAGING FEES

If you're not careful, you can be "fee'd" to death. OK, that's an overstatement, but fees do take a big bite out of your portfolio.

Assume that you are an employee with 35 years until retirement and a current 401(k) account balance of $25,000. If your returns during the next 35 years average 7 percent and fees and expenses reduce your average returns by 0.5 percent, your account balance will grow to $227,000 at retirement, even if there are no further contributions to your account.

If fees and expenses are 1.5 percent, however, your account balance will reach only $163,000. The 1 percent difference in fees and expenses reduces your account balance at retirement by 28 percent.

Source: http://www.dol.gov/ebsa/
publications/401k_employee.html

DOUBLE DOWN

Figuring out how long it will take for your investment to double is easier than you think thanks to a mathematical rule named The Rule of 72. Here's the calculation:

Years to double = 72 divided by the interest rate (compounding annually)

For example, if you want your money to double in eight years, you need to earn an interest rate of 9 percent. (72 divided by 9 equals 8.) If you are earning 6 percent interest, it takes 12 years for your money to double.

The Stock Market Game

Are you curious about the stock market but lack funds to invest? The Stock Market Game gives you a virtual windfall of $100,000 to build a mock portfolio you manage online. Schools usually sponsor the game, which lets you team up with friends to build your portfolio and market knowledge.

Other stock market simulators are available outside of school. Check out Wall Street Survivor online.

Here Today, Gone Tomorrow

If you were a kid years ago, you'd head to Woolworths for the latest toy or school clothes. Wool-what? Exactly. There is risk in owning stock of a company. Even the seemingly most secure companies can be taken over by other companies or can file for bankruptcy. Nothing is forever, as this list of once-prominent companies shows. That's one reason why diversification is so important.

Woolworths (1879–1997)
Montgomery Ward (1872–2000)
Pan Am Airlines (1927–1991)
Borders Books and Music (1971–2001)
Circuit City (1984–2009)

GET READY, GET SET, SAVE!

You've learned about the institutions, methods, people, and tools that will make your money grow through saving. Your next step is a simple one. Start saving. It doesn't matter how much. Any little amount will do. Save in a way so that you're true to yourself.

Understand your risk tolerance. And come up with a plan to invest for the future. Follow this advice and you'll have a good start on the path to wealth.

GLOSSARY

401(k)—a retirement account offered by an employer that provides tax incentives for using it

bond—a certificate issued by a corporation or government to raise money; the issuer pays interest on the bond to the lender for a certain amount of time and then returns the principal to the lender

credit union—a not-for-profit financial institution set up by members of a group

diversification—concept of putting money into various types of investments, such as stocks, bonds, cash, and real estate

index—an imaginary portfolio of securities representing a particular market; stock and bond indexes are used to construct index mutual funds

inertia—law of physics stating that a body at rest remains at rest unless acted on by an external force

inflation—an economic state in which prices of goods and services continue to rise

interest—a fee charged to borrow money; interest is usually calculated as a percentage of the amount borrowed or lent

mutual fund—savings tool that pools money from multiple investors for the purpose of buying a variety of investments

principal—original amount invested or the amount borrowed or still owed on a loan, separate from interest

return—amount of money earned on a particular investment, typically represented as a percentage

risk tolerance—amount of risk a person is willing to handle

stock—value of a company, divided into shares when sold to investors

time horizon—length of time of an investment; time horizon can range from days to years

ADDITIONAL RESOURCES

FURTHER READING

Bateman, Katherine Roberta. *The Young Investor: Projects and Activities for Making Your Money Grow.* Chicago: Chicago Review Press, 2010.

Blumenthal, Karen. *The Wall Street Journal Guide to Starting Your Financial Life.* New York: Three Rivers Press, 2009.

Gagne, Tammy. *A Teen Guide to Saving and Investing.* Hockessin, Del.: Mitchell Lane Publishers, 2014.

Mooney, Carla. *Smart Savings and Financial Planning.* New York: Rosen Pub., 2013.

INTERNET SITES

Use FactHound to find Internet sites related to this book. All of the sites on FactHound have been researched by our staff.

Here's all you do:

Visit *www.facthound.com*

Type in this code:
9780756549220

OTHER SITES TO EXPLORE:

The Internet Guide to Funding College and Section 529 Savings Plans
http://www.savingforcollege.com/

The Mint
http://www.themint.org

Practical Money Skills
http://www.practicalmoneyskills.com

Choose to Save. 7 May 2014.
http://www.choosetosave.org

Consumer Financial Protection
Bureau. 7 May 2014.
http://www.consumerfinance.gov

Credit Union National Association.
7 May 2014. http://www.cuna.org

Farrell, Chris. *The New Frugality.*
New York: Bloomsbury Press, 2010.

Finaid! Financial Aid, College
Scholarships and Student Loans.
7 May 2014. http://www.finaid.org

Financial Industry Regulatory
Authority. 7 May 2014.
http://www.finra.org

Foreign Policy Association.
7 May 2014. http://www.fpa.org

Franklin, Benjamin. *Franklin's Way to
Wealth, or Poor Richard Improved.* New
York: Samuel Wood & Sons, 1820.

Franklin Institute. 7 May 2014.
https://www.fi.edu

The Internet Guide to Funding
College and Section 529 Savings
Plans. 7 May 2014.
http://www.savingforcollege.com/

The Mint: Fun Financial Literacy
Activities for Kids, Teens, Parents
and Teachers. 7 May 2014.
http://www.themint.org

National Endowment for Financial
Education. 7 May 2014.
http://www.nefe.org

Practical Money Skills: Financial
Literacy for Everyone. 7 May 2014.
http://www.practicalmoneyskills.
com

Robin, Vicki, and Joe Dominguez.
*Your Money or Your Life: 9 Steps
to Transforming Your Relationship
with Money and Achieving Financial
Independence.* New York: Penguin
Books, 2008.

Tobias, Andrew P. *The Only
Investment Guide You'll Ever Need.*
Boston: Mariner Books/Houghton
Mifflin Harcourt, 2010.

United States Department of Labor.
7 May 2014. http://www.dol.gov

Wall Street Survivor. 8 May 2014.
http://www.wallstreetsurvivor.com

Yahoo! Finance. 7 May 2014.
http://finance.yahoo.com

SOURCE NOTES

Page 22: E-mail interview.
21 Aug. 2013.

Page 26: E-mail interview.
26 Aug. 2013.

Page 28: Benjamin Franklin. *The Way
to Wealth.* 9 May 2014. http://www.
bartleby.com/400/prose/351.html

About the Author

Kara McGuire is an award-winning personal finance writer, consumer researcher, and speaker. She writes a personal finance column for the Minneapolis *Star Tribune* and formerly worked for the public radio program *Marketplace Money*. She enjoys teaching young people and parents about money. Kara lives in St. Paul, Minnesota, with her husband, Matt, and children Charlotte, Teddy, and August.